This book belongs to:

●●●●●●●●●●●●●●●●●●●●

1

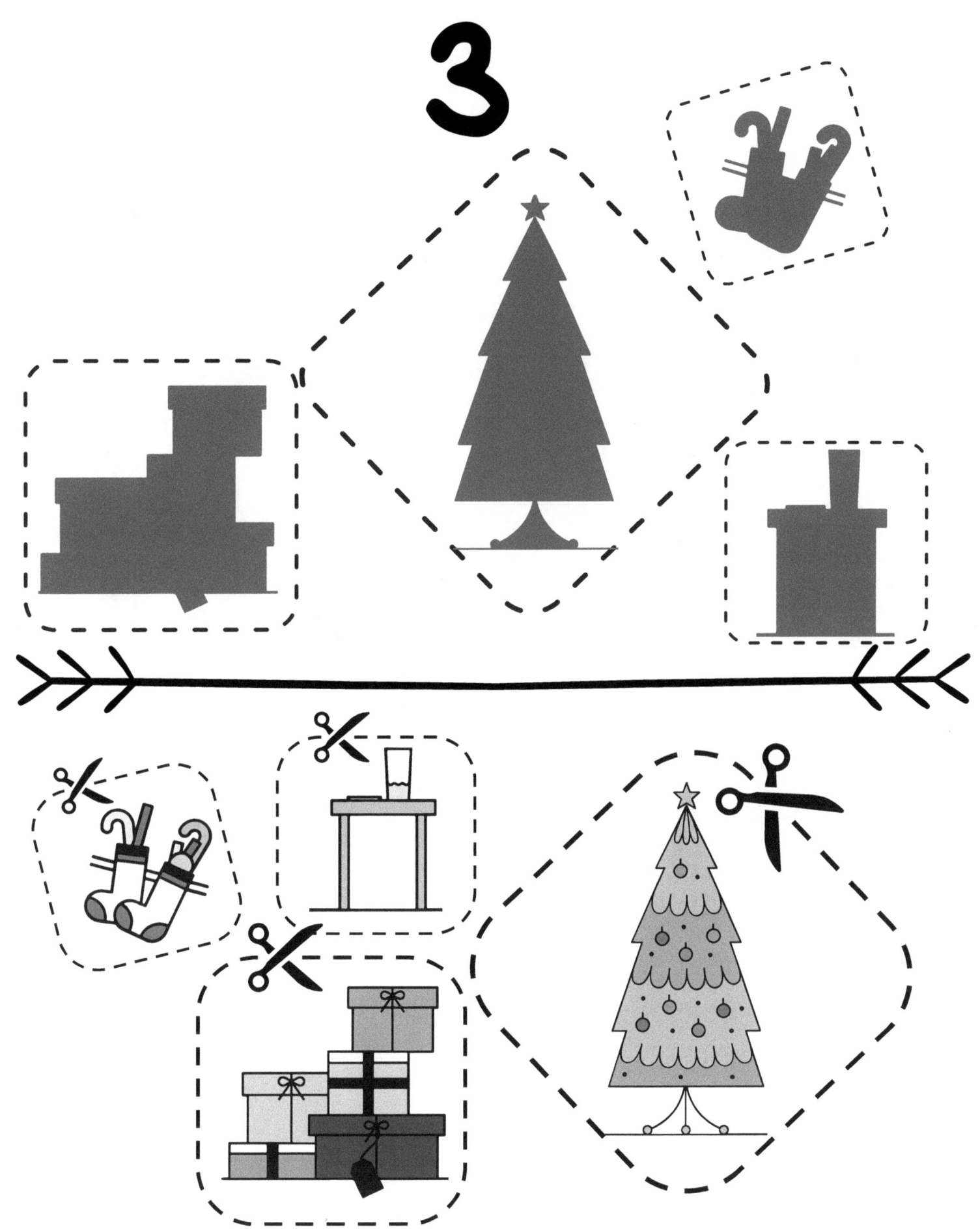

1

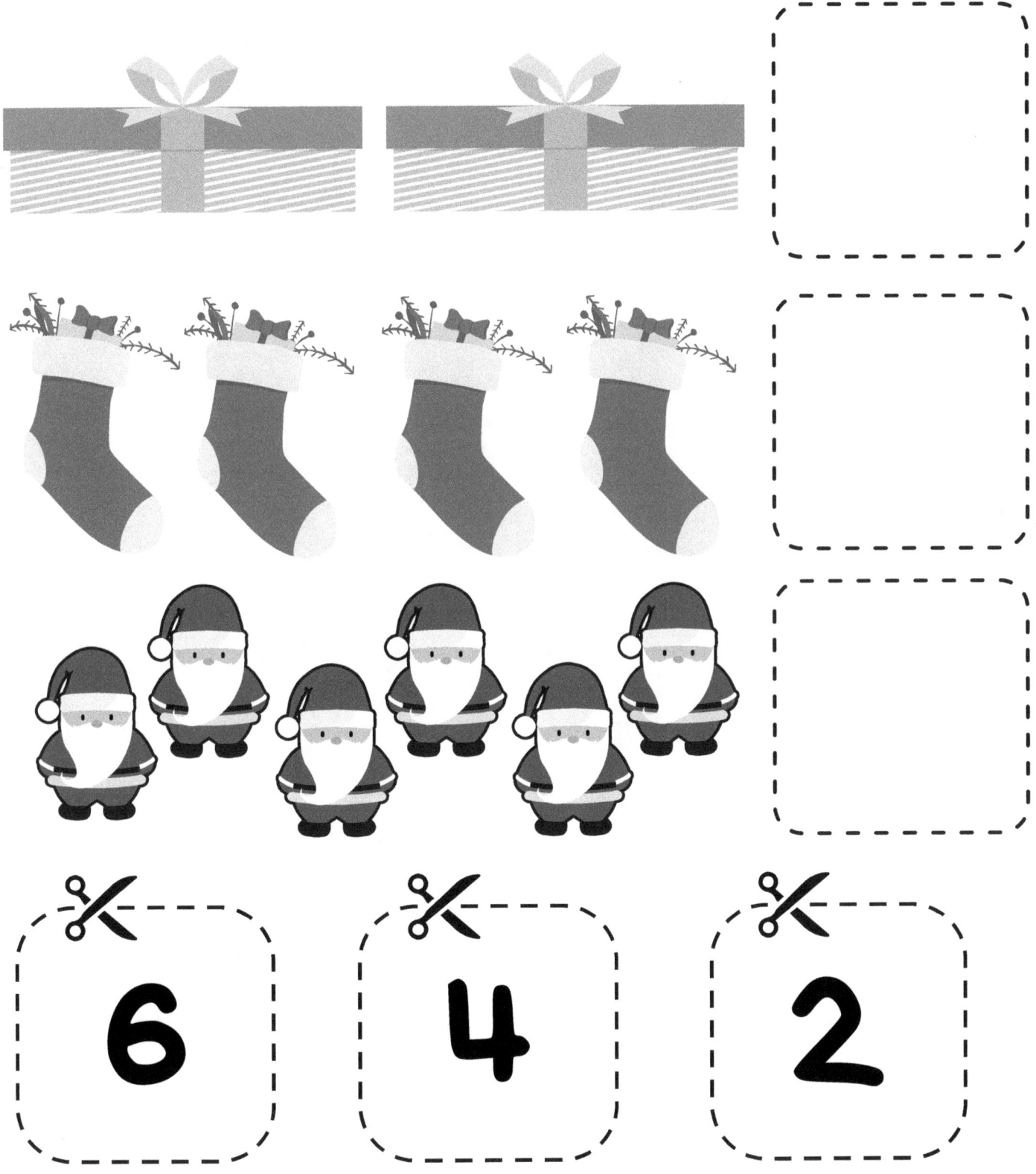

2

7

2

3

3

1

2

3

1

2

3

There are ☐ raindeers

3 6 2 5

There are [ ] Christmas trees

2 5 4 3

There are [ ] snowmen

9 5 7 3

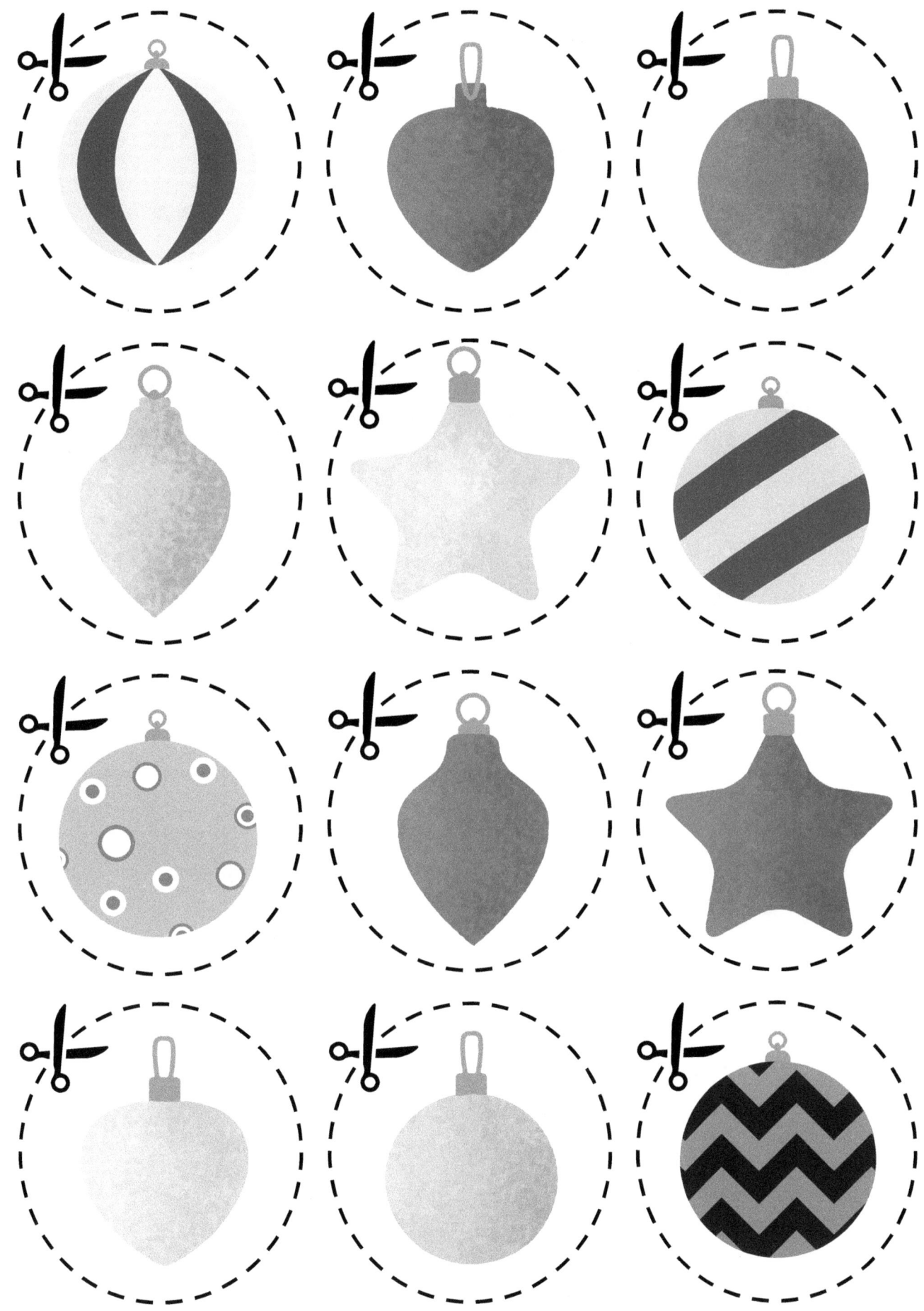

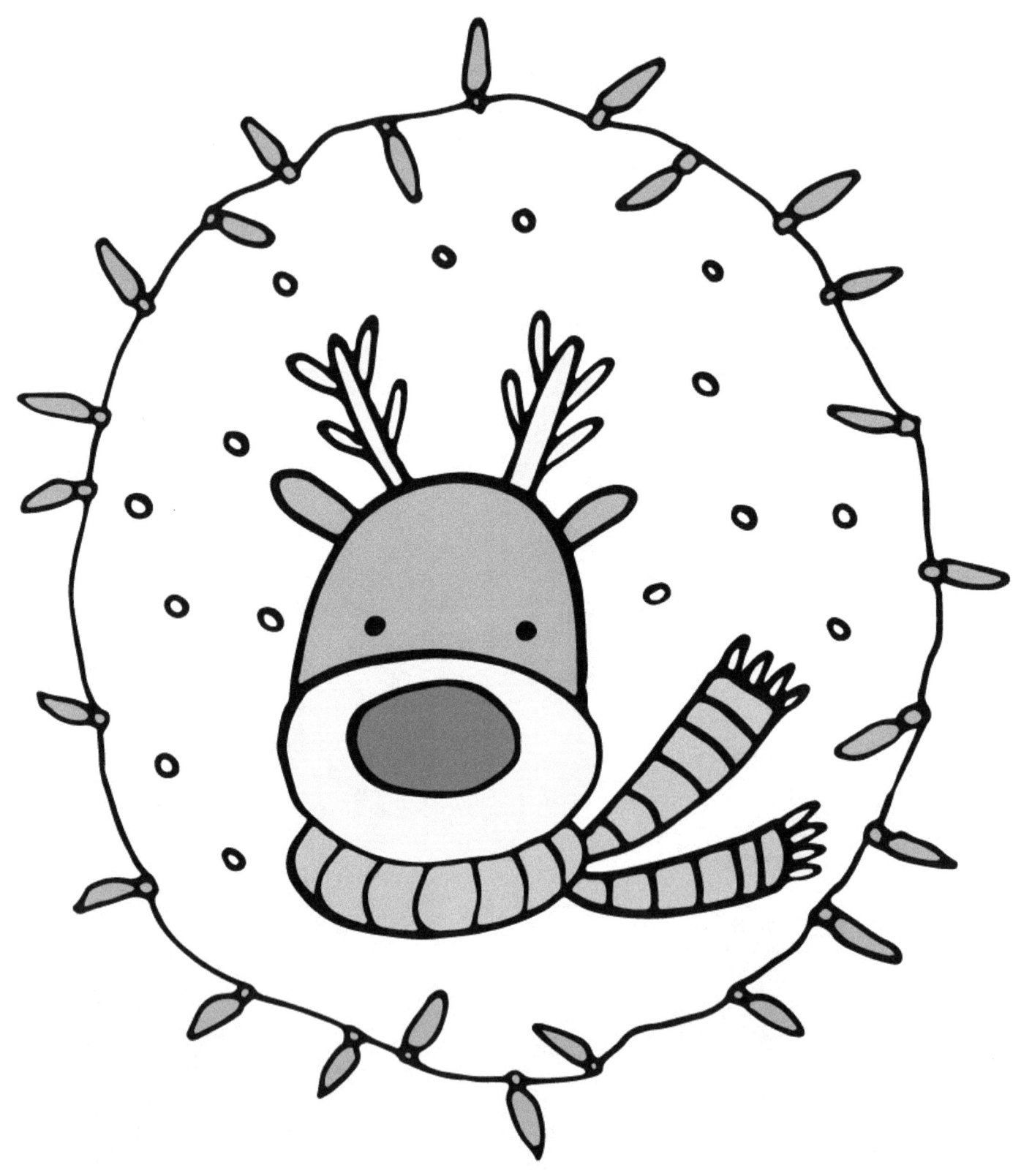

HAPPY HOLIDAYS

CPSIA information can be obtained
at www.ICGtesting.com
Printed in the USA
BVHW052140041121
620856BV00017B/203

9 798576 006656